BROADWAY PLA████████ ██C.

To Gillian
on Her
37th Birthday

by

Michael Brady

249 WEST 29 STREET NEW YORK NY 10001 (212) 563-3820

To Gillian on Her 37th Birthday

First printing: September 1984
ISBN: 0-88145-022-7

Cover Art by Marguerite Woolf
Design by Marie Donovan
Set in Baskerville by Techna-Type, York, PA.
Printed and bound by BookCrafters, Inc., Chelsea, MI

For Patricia

CIRCLE IN THE SQUARE

(DOWNTOWN) — 159 BLEECKER STREET — 254-6330

M SQUARE ENTERTAINMENT, INC.
Mitchell Maxwell, Alan J. Schuster, Fred H. Krones

and

THE ENSEMBLE STUDIO THEATRE

Curt Dempster
Artistic Director

David S. Rosenak
Managing Director

present

TO GILLIAN ON HER 37TH BIRTHDAY

by

MICHAEL BRADY

with

FRANCES CONROY	JEAN De BAER
RICHMOND HOXIE	CHERYL McFADDEN
NOELLE PARKER	SARAH JESSICA PARKER

DAVID RASCHE

Scenery by	*Lights by*	*Costumes by*
ROBERT THAYER	**ALLEN LEE HUGHES**	**DEBORAH SHAW**
Sound by	*Production Stage Manager*	*Music Composed by*
BRUCE ELLMAN	**RICHARD COSTABILE**	**ROBERT DENNIS**

Associate Producer
ANDREW R. MORSE

Directed by

PAMELA BERLIN

CAST

(in order of appearance)

David . . . . DAVID RASCHE

Rachel . . . . SARAH JESSICA PARKER

Cindy . . . . NOËLLE PARKER

Kevin . . . . FRANCES CONROY

Paul . . . . RICHMOND HOXIE

Esther . . . . JEAN DE BAER

Gillian . . . . CHERYL McFADDEN

SETTING

A small island off the coast of New England.

TIME

A weekend in August.

UNDERSTUDIES
Understudies never substitute for listed players unless a specific announcement
for the appearance is made at the time of the performance.
For Cindy, Rachel, Kevin—Kerstin Kilgo.

THERE WILL BE ONE TEN-MINUTE INTERMISSION.

ORIGINAL PRODUCTION NOTES

To Gillian on Her 37th Birthday opened at the Ensemble Studio Theatre on November 2, 1983. The cast members were the same as those appearing in the Circle in the Square production (see Playbill on previous pages; opening date: March 22, 1984) with the exception of:

David   James Rebhorn
Kevin   Heather Lupton

Michael Brady's first play, *Sara,* was produced by Equity Library Theatre. *Korczak's Children,* based on the life of child psychologist and Holocaust victim Janusz Korczak, has received readings at The Ensemble Studio Theatre and the American Jewish Theatre, and was named the first annual winner of the Gesu Award in Playwriting for 1982. *To Gillian on Her 37th Birthday* was developed through the literary department of The Ensemble and was featured in their *New Voices* in the spring of 1983. Mr. Brady is a member of The Ensemble Studio Theatre and is a recipient of a 1984 New York State Creative Artists' Program grant.

To Gillian on Her 37th Birthday is a play in two acts. The time is the present. The place is the back deck and beach of David's island home. The action traces the final weekend of August.

CHARACTERS

DAVID, age 37, a college professor, temporarily retired

RACHEL, age 16, David's daughter

CINDY, age 16, Rachel's friend

PAUL, age 38, David's brother-in-law, married to Esther

ESTHER, age 39, David's sister-in-law, a psychologist, married to Paul

KEVIN, age 28, friend of Paul and Esther, recently divorced

GILLIAN, age 35, David's former wife who died in a sailing accident two years prior to the events of the play; Esther's sister

ACT ONE

Scene One

(From darkness, the outline of the northern sky at night, after moon fall. Bands of stars in luminous progression. Gradually the star light reveals a stretch of beach. In the background, a weathered house with a wooden deck. To one side of the house is a small weather station—thermometer, barometer, wind gauge, and a rain bucket. Built into the wall is a small ledge with a log and a pencil. Sitting on the beach and looking skyward are DAVID, late thirties, RACHEL, his daughter, sixteen, and CINDY, also sixteen. All are in casual clothes—sweatshirts and sneakers. It is after midnight, in August.)

DAVID: How long now?

RACHEL: *(Shines a small flashlight on her wrist.)* Twenty-four minutes.

DAVID: One for every hour of the day . . . Well, let's give it a little longer. You can't rush these things.

CINDY: Where's Perseus again? *(Per-soos)*

DAVID: *(Correcting her pronunciation.)* Pear-see-us.

CINDY: Pear-see-us.

DAVID: *(Pointing)* Right there.

CINDY: And that's where our meteors come from?

RACHEL: No, that's where they appear to come from.

DAVID: Correctly qualified.

CINDY: *(Reaching for a large map of the heavens.)* Can I chart it?

RACHEL: You'd better let me chart that one.

CINDY: I'll do it.

RACHEL: It's kind of complicated.

CINDY: I can do it.

DAVID: (*To* CINDY) Do you know what's special, what's very special about these meteors?

CINDY: (*Still working the chart.*) What?

DAVID: They come back at the same time, year after year. In fact, a certain young person got launched under this very meteor shower.

RACHEL: Daddy!

DAVID: Accidently, of course.

RACHEL: You're embarrassing me.

DAVID: Now don't be a prude, Rachel. Cindy is as good as family.

CINDY: (*To* RACHEL) Hey, we all have to start somewhere. They tell me I happened in a jeep.

DAVID: You see? (*Pause*) All right, drum roll please . . . (CINDY *provides this.*) This year's meteor shower is officially . . . over. (*As they all begin to move.*) Wait. Don't move. Can't you hear that? Listèn. The waves . . . the waves are talking to us.

RACHEL: Daddy . . .

DAVID: Listen . . . the waves are communicating. They are saying it's time. . . .

RACHEL: What are you doing?

DAVID: Rachel, just calm down. Everything is under control, all right? The waves are saying . . . it's time . . . time for Cindy's quiz.

CINDY: Funny, I missed that.

DAVID: Come on. (CINDY *crosses to the telescope.*) Now, find the summer triangle.

CINDY: (*Looking through view finder.*) Got it.

DAVID: The top star of the triangle, pulsing ever so slightly?

CINDY: That's Vega.

DAVID: And what's special about Vega?

CINDY: Recently discovered evidence of a new solar system.

DAVID: Yes! There are planets up there! New worlds springing to life, even as we speak. Think about that, just for a minute. It's all happening again, the same glorious business. Another Jupiter, a new Saturn with her rings of crystal and ice. And it has always been right in front of us, but we couldn't see. We are here to create new life! That is the message of Vega. But we forget. We lack vision. Just look at what passes for our literature. Have you looked at our literature lately?

CINDY: I've been pretty busy lately. . . .

DAVID: Well, I'm depending on you. You will be the next creators. Hold on to the eternals! Watch out for all this feeling business. You and me and what are you feeling, and I'm feeling and blah, blah, blah. Look to that which endures. The sea, the sky, the stars, memory, and the human heart. These are the eternals . . .

CINDY: Right. . . .

RACHEL: Daddy, come back. Daddy!

DAVID: Where were we?

RACHEL: Cindy's quiz.

CINDY: (To RACHEL) Thank you.

DAVID: What do we call the brightest star in the constellation?

CINDY: The alpha.

DAVID: The alpha . . . (Pointing skyward.) Who is that fellow?

CINDY: Sirius. In the constellation of the dog, arf, arf.

DAVID: And what's special about Sirius, arf, arf?

CINDY: Sirius is the brightest star in the sky, the alpha of the alphas.

DAVID: You're on a roll. Show me where the morning star will rise.

CINDY: (*Points low on the horizon.*) Right there.

DAVID: And what's incorrect about "Morning Star"?

CINDY: It's not a star. It's Venus, which is a planet.

DAVID: That was terrific, really. Excellent. I don't see why you don't make A's.

CINDY: I lack motivation.

DAVID: Well, keep at it. You never know when they'll bring back College Bowl. Quick recall . . .

CINDY: . . . of specific fact. I think I'll take my chances. (*A wave breaks against the shore, quite loud.*)

DAVID: Oh, that was a nice one. When the surf got wild and crazy like this, your mother used to come down here and wail like a Banshee. You remember? (*Pause*) Am I talking in a vacuum?

RACHEL: I remember, Daddy. I was down by High Surf today. There was this guy . . .

DAVID: What? Now you know the rules. I don't want you swimming at High Surf Beach.

RACHEL: I didn't go in the water.

DAVID: There's an undertow. And there's no lifeguard. You don't go to any unauthorized beaches.

RACHEL: I was just talking to this guy.

DAVID: Not at High Surf.

RACHEL: All right.

CINDY: (*Pointing skyward.*) What do you call that one?

DAVID: That big red one we call Aldebaron.

CINDY: Is that like Al de Baron of England or something?

DAVID: No, but good try. Aldebaron is a Persian word. It means "the follower."

CINDY: Oh yeah?

DAVID: Yeah. And if that doesn't meet your fancy, we can rename it. For each generation must rediscover the universe. Yeats said that. Or maybe it was Joyce . . . Anyway, for Aldebaron let's say Ward. And we'll call that one June. And that one Wally . . . And that little rascal over there? No? That's the Beaver.

CINDY: What is he talking about?

RACHEL: My father is being involved. It's an old TV show.

CINDY: (*To* DAVID) You are really heavy into daytime television.

DAVID: Guilty.

CINDY: Well, watch it. Too much of that stuff can make you sterile. And you wouldn't want that.

DAVID: Heaven forbid. (*Crossing to* RACHEL, *who is looking through the telescope.*) You will be relieved to know, Rachel, that in your absence the stars have not shifted in their orbits.

RACHEL: I wasn't gone that long.

DAVID: Two months? Reminded me of the old days. Your mother off in Sumatra or the Serengeti, or the San Diego Zoo, an orangoutang under each arm. Waiting for the summer to end and Gil to come back to us, dirty and happy. Except this year it was me   and Cindy, waiting for you to come back. (*Pause*) Where's your mother's hat?

RACHEL: What?

DAVID: Her hat. Her lucky special hat. I've been looking for it.

RACHEL: It's around.

DAVID: Where?

RACHEL: I don't know. Around. Somewhere.

DAVID: You've seen it?

RACHEL: No, but it's got to be in the house somewhere.

DAVID: Having spent the worse part of four days taking the

house apart drawer by drawer, I think I can say your mother's hat is not around in the house somewhere. You haven't passed the hat along to your aunt?

RACHEL: Daddy, I didn't take Mommy's hat. And Aunt Esther would never take something that didn't belong to her.

DAVID: I'm just trying to ensure that your mother's hat doesn't end up in the trash. Is that so terrible? Rachel, you are beginning to pick up some of your aunt's less appealing characteristics. You two must have had some interesting conversations. What to do if Daddy's acting a little strange when you get back, especially as we get near the anniversary of you-know-what.

RACHEL: Daddy, you've got to learn to discharge.

DAVID: Discharge? Oh, really?

RACHEL: Yeah.

DAVID: Learn to discharge? Now that is the voice of Esther. I do not have to learn anything, young lady. And I hope you're prepared to play the host tomorrow, because I am not.

CINDY: I just saw one!

DAVID: Where? (CINDY points) Wrong quadrant.

CINDY: I really did, honest.

DAVID: No, not official.

CINDY: How come you always decide what's official?

DAVID: Knowledge is power. (Turning back to RACHEL.) Rachel, I have been what is called a good sport to this point. Tell me who is coming tomorrow with Esther and Paul, just tell me who this surprise visitor is. That would be very adult of you.

RACHEL: Yeah, but then if I told you, it wouldn't be a surprise.

DAVID: Not funny, Rachel. Now listen to me. If your mother were here, she would explain to you that most mammals, and that includes us, mate for life. And it is not uncommon for the surviving mate to remain . . . apart, after the death of his companion, and that mourning for two years, or for a lifetime, is an accepted part of the natural world, despite what your aunt might tell you. I expected better of you. I really did. (*Long pause*)

CINDY: (*To* DAVID) Do you know what it's called when there are a lot of waves all together? Hey, I'm talking to you.

DAVID: Cindy?

CINDY: That's what they call me. Remember you said one night . . . an exaltation of nightingales, right? So what's a "blank" of waves? A lot of waves, all bunched up?

DAVID: I am at a loss.

CINDY: This is an official stump?

DAVID: Official.

CINDY: My first stump. A girl always remembers her first. You ready? A lot of waves all bunched up is called, ta da, a roost.

DAVID: A roost.

CINDY: And if a wave is real long, like the one we saw last February, you call that the fetch of the wave.

DAVID: (*Laughs*) The fetch.

CINDY: Precisely.

DAVID: The fetch of a wave. That's very nice. And it's also very late. (*To* CINDY) Run tomorrow?

RACHEL: It's supposed to be very hot tomorrow.

DAVID: Don't nag, Rachel. (*To* CINDY) Fetch me early while it's still cool.

CINDY: I'll . . . roost you out. (*Starts to go.*) Well, goodnight.

DAVID: Goodnight, Cindy.

(CINDY *and* RACHEL *walk off a small distance, then stop.*)

RACHEL: Fetches and roosts?

CINDY: I'm sorry. I was running out of diversions. He likes to talk about waves.

RACHEL: He likes to talk about anything.

CINDY: Waves especially. So I read this book.

RACHEL: Oh, you read a book! Wo!

CINDY: Don't go all razors on me.

RACHEL: I'm sorry. God, you heard him going at me. And why is he talking about the hat?

CINDY: I don't know. He likes to talk. Sometimes he gets a little carried away.

RACHEL: He stares into space, at nothing. And he talks to himself.

CINDY: Everybody talks to themselves.

RACHEL: This is different.

CINDY: So I'll stay over.

RACHEL: No.

CINDY: What's the big deal?

RACHEL: No big deal, but no.

CINDY: Sure. So who is this mystery woman, person, thing, it, anyway?

RACHEL: My lips are sealed.

CINDY: Come on.

RACHEL: We'll all be nice and relaxed tomorrow, Cindy.

CINDY: I'm going home right now and put on my nice face.

RACHEL: Now just don't pull anything, you've promised, okay? Don't let him run too much. And if he gets wobbly . . .

CINDY: . . . I'll sit on him, promise.

RACHEL: By the way, it's an exaltation of larks.

CINDY: He said nightingales.

RACHEL: He's wrong. It happens.

CINDY: I am crushed.

(CINDY *exits.* RACHEL *returns to* DAVID, *who is busy with his star charts.*)

RACHEL: This boy I met at the beach today. He's pretty interesting. (*Pause*)

DAVID: Sorry, kiddo, I just went vacant. What was that?

RACHEL: Nothing. No big deal.

DAVID: Come on now. Out with it.

RACHEL: Nothing.

DAVID: It sounded more like a something.

RACHEL: This boy on the beach, he talked about cybernetics. I didn't know what he meant.

DAVID: Cybernetics . . . robots, artificial intelligence, like me. You want to study all that?

RACHEL: No, Daddy.

DAVID: I guess it would be engineering, for the basics, and math, logic, and programming . . .

RACHEL: I said no! I just wanted to know what the word meant.

DAVID: Sorry, I guess I'm not listening. Your mother always said that was my worst fault.

RACHEL: Don't be mad about tomorrow.

DAVID: I'm not mad.

RACHEL: This is me you're talking to.

DAVID: Annoyed, maybe.

RACHEL: Then don't be annoyed maybe. Daddy, when you meet somebody in a social situation, you don't have to do anything, unless you want to.

DAVID: Aren't I supposed to be saying this to you?

RACHEL: You did, last year. It was terrific advice. I recommend it. (*Pause*) Don't stay up too late.

DAVID: I won't.

RACHEL: I miss her, too, every day. (*Pause*) Cindy's been keeping the star charts?

DAVID: Uh-hmm.

RACHEL: I thought I was the official star chart keeper.

DAVID: You are . . .

RACHEL: Always and forever.

DAVID: . . . But when the official keeper is away, we give the unofficial keeper some practice.

RACHEL: Did you miss me?

DAVID: Of course I missed you. (*Pause*)

RACHEL: Don't forget to take your potassium pills.

DAVID: Would I do that?

RACHEL: I mean it. You take them or I'll tell Aunt Esther.

DAVID: Ah, there's my modern version of the Apocalypse. (*Reaches into pocket, pulls out bottle of pills, takes one out. Moves hands around.*) Pick the hand with the pill! Just twenty wins yuh fifty, twenty wins yuh fifty.

RACHEL: (*Picks a hand.*) The pill.

DAVID: (*Moving hands again.*) Pick the lucky hand . . .

RACHEL: Cut it out. (DAVID *swallows the pill.*) Aren't you coming in?

DAVID: In a minute.

RACHEL: It's getting late.

DAVID: Let's not get started again, Rachel.

RACHEL: Please come in with me.

DAVID: I'll see you in the morning. (RACHEL *exits*) Good night. (DAVID *listens to the waves breaking against the shore.*) Gil, Gil? Tonight? Please? I'm forgetting the details. (*Slowly a thin arc of light moves across the stage and fades,* DAVID *following the falling star with his finger.*) Gil. (*Closing his eyes.*) I wish I may, I wish I might, but oh, God, I'm certain I won't have the wish I wish tonight.

(*Stage lights gradually fade.*)

Scene Two

(*The following morning.* KEVIN *and* PAUL *are staring at the water.* PAUL *is in his late thirties.* KEVIN *is younger, late twenties.*)

KEVIN: Beautiful. Exactly as you promised.

PAUL: You see?

KEVIN: Now stop holding out on me.

PAUL: Kevin, would I do that?

KEVIN: Don't do the charm number either.

PAUL: You're just nervous about meeting an available male.

KEVIN: I am nervous, but that's not what's wrong.

PAUL: You were the same way on your blind date with that guy who wanted to mass produce gerbils as an alternative food source.

KEVIN: David is not a blind date. The two of you are sitting on something. I would like some details.

PAUL: (*Growls*) Esther gave you the details.

KEVIN: Esther told me "boating accident."

PAUL: We were on their boat. Clear skies, no small-craft warnings. David was at the wheel, or whatever you call those things. Gillian was half-way up the mast. She liked to do things like that, drove me half crazy. . . . We hit something. Submerged debris. Gil fell and hit her head on the deck. An accident, Kevin.

KEVIN: Why are you making this so difficult? There is something else.

PAUL: This was two years ago, and. . . .

KEVIN: And?

PAUL: And it was also Gillian's birthday. Which is also tomorrow.

KEVIN: Oh, Paul.

PAUL: We didn't even think it all out till just a few days ago. And we thought you would have backed out.

KEVIN: I would have.

PAUL: And we thought that would be a waste of a perfectly decent weekend.

KEVIN: Paul . . .

PAUL: Just relax.

KEVIN: I hate it when you tell me to relax. Did it ever occur to you that I don't need the competition, that maybe I don't need to be compared to that overgrown golden retriever he was married to?

PAUL: Oh. (ESTHER *appears at the door.*)

ESTHER: (*To* PAUL) You may think I enjoy unloading the car by myself. You would be wrong. (*To* KEVIN) Not you. (ESTHER *exits.*)

PAUL: (*Starting to exit.*) Why don't you just concentrate on all that water? I'm told it has a soothing effect, though it's never done a thing for me.

KEVIN: Paul . . .

PAUL: Concentrate. I'm prepared to put that in writing.

(PAUL *exits.* KEVIN *concentrates on the water. After a beat,* CINDY *enters, jogging. She stops, stretches, oblivious to* KEVIN, *then runs toward the deck.*)

KEVIN: Rachel. Hello!

CINDY: (*Slowing down*) No. I'm not Rachel . . . I'm a friend of Rachel's.

KEVIN: Ah. My name is Kevin.

CINDY: Oh?

KEVIN: I'm with Paul and Esther. Do you know . . .

CINDY: Sure. Got it. (*Crossing to* KEVIN, *shaking hands.*) I'm Cindy. No one's here.

KEVIN: We noticed.

CINDY: Rachel's at the supermarket. She's into that stuff.

KEVIN: And David?

CINDY: He's still jogging. South side by now. We usually pace each other. You know Mr. . . . You know David?

KEVIN: Yes. I took a lot of his courses in college, years and years ago.

CINDY: Oh, so you're the one.

KEVIN: He's talked about me?

CINDY: No. (*Pause*) He doesn't teach any more.

KEVIN: Well, maybe he'll get back to it. (*Pause*)

CINDY: He didn't think you'd be here this early.

KEVIN: We'll surprise him, then.

CINDY: (*Starts to run off.*) I don't think he's all that fond of surprises.

(PAUL *enters from the house.*)

PAUL: (*To* CINDY) Hi, muscles. (CINDY *stops, puts one foot behind her head and turns.*)

CINDY: Hello, Mr. Cerebellum.

PAUL: (*Exaggerated*) "Cerebellum," score one for the tyke. Have you two met?

CINDY: Check. I'll tell . . . David you're here.

KEVIN: No need.

CINDY: No problem. Oh, don't worry . . . (*Starts to exit, stops.*) I won't spoil your surprise. (CINDY *exits.*)

KEVIN: The kid next door?

PAUL: You got it.

KEVIN: She didn't seem overjoyed to meet me. Or is that just the charming aloofness of the natives?

PAUL: She's all right. A little hormonal at times, but all right.

KEVIN: This is the wrong time to be doing this.

PAUL: You're not doing anything, except getting away for a few days.

KEVIN: I go back tonight.

PAUL: Would you stop? You're our guest, now start acting the part.

(ESTHER *enters from the house, late thirties, dressed for the beach. She crosses to them, sniffs the air.*)

ESTHER: Did I tell you or did I tell you?

KEVIN: You told me.

ESTHER: You bottle it, take it back and sell it. It's that good. (*Breathing*) Come on, let's do it. In good stuff, out shit. In good, out shit.

KEVIN: I'm going to explore a bit.

PAUL: Come back. (KEVIN *smiles and slowly walks off.*)

ESTHER: In good, out shit.

PAUL: Would you stop?

ESTHER: Would you take that burr out of your behind?

PAUL: You have the potential here for real disaster.

ESTHER: You want to not use your mystic tone of voice?

PAUL: Esther, the potential for real, honest, nice people disaster.

ESTHER: Just what are we doing? Kevin wants to meet men. She asks you; we arrange. End of story.

PAUL: Not quite, Esther, not quite the end of the story. We didn't just happen to forget tomorrow is Gil's birthday, we didn't just casually overlook the most traumatic event in all of our lives.

ESTHER: Are you through? Kevin can take care of herself. She's a big girl.

PAUL: I'm talking about David.

ESTHER: You are always mouthing off that you are his oldest friend. You could do something, you know, instead of criticizing.

PAUL: I'll handle it in my own way.

ESTHER: Look, Kevin is here, so let's just make the best of it, shall we, Mr. Negativity?

PAUL: You're bulldozing, Esther.

ESTHER: Such a charming, subtly hostile, faintly masculine choice of phrase, bull dozing.

PAUL: You are bulldozing, and I'm letting you get away with it.

(RACHEL *enters. She puts down a bag of groceries and crosses to them.*)

RACHEL: Hi, hi, hi. How's your dog?

ESTHER: Good, how's your dog?

RACHEL: Good.

PAUL: (*Examining bag.*) What's all this?

RACHEL: We call it food, sahib.

PAUL: We can get the food, we have the car.

RACHEL: I have the bike.

ESTHER: She's self-reliant. What'd I tell you?

RACHEL: I like to do the errands. You two shouldn't have to worry about anything while you're here.

ESTHER: You hear that? It's her way or the highway, right?

RACHEL: Right.

ESTHER: It's in the blood. Well, let me look at you.

RACHEL: Okay. (RACHEL *twirls around.*)

ESTHER: Did you miss us?

RACHEL: Yeah. You miss me?

ESTHER and PAUL: Yeah.

ESTHER: How you doing, let me have it.

RACHEL: I don't know. He keeps running, all the time.

PAUL: All that health, bad for you.

ESTHER: Shut up.

RACHEL: I try to get him to take his potassium, but he makes me feel like a nurse or something.

ESTHER: You know, I asked how you are, not how's Daddy. . . .

RACHEL: Yeah, right. There's this boy.

PAUL: Ah hah, back a week and already you've got a boyfriend.

RACHEL: I don't have a boyfriend, Uncle Paul. I am eyeballing a boyfriend.

ESTHER: He likes? (RACHEL *shrugs.*) He talks?

RACHEL: He talks.

ESTHER: That's something. Are you involved? Nothing is a problem. You need help?

RACHEL: (*Laughs*) No, it's not that. I don't even know his name.

PAUL: Doesn't mean a thing.

ESTHER: (*To* PAUL) Your mouth. (*To* RACHEL) You talk to me, I mean it. Morning, noon, or night. Sex, biology, babies, no babies.

RACHEL: Aunt Esther . . .

ESTHER: The works, you hear me?

RACHEL: I'm okay on biology. It's all the other stuff.

PAUL: What other stuff?

RACHEL: I just want things to be . . . normal, you know? Quiet? And Daddy . . .

ESTHER: Look kiddo, David, I love him, I do, but when he starts talking anal-sphinctereze, no one can put up with him. So you leave him to me.

PAUL: Esther . . .

ESTHER: Shhh.

RACHEL: He thinks you took Mommy's hat.

ESTHER: What?

RACHEL: Or he thinks I did. He's out here every night, sometimes all night . . .

(DAVID *enters, running. He stops, begins to stretch.* CINDY *enters a few steps behind.*)

PAUL: David!

ESTHER: Hello, David. Hi, Cindy.

DAVID: Well, the same old cast of characters.

ESTHER: How are you, David?

DAVID: We're not playing the dating game today? Don't tell me there's been a sudden outbreak of good taste.

PAUL: There is someone we'd like you to meet . . .

DAVID: Then it is to be Christians and lions. All right, let's get this over with. Where is she? (*To* CINDY) In the trunk, I hope, gasping for air?

PAUL: David . . .

RACHEL: (*To* ESTHER) You see? He's been like this all week.

DAVID: Oh he has, has he? (*To* ESTHER, *throwing his towel down on the deck.*) Getting little updates from the front?

ESTHER: Let's just slow down and take this back to step one. How are you, David?

DAVID: I am fine, Esther, how are you? And I am well-tuned emotionally, despite obvious stories to the contrary.

RACHEL: Daddy, I do not tell stories.

DAVID: (*Stretching, not looking at* RACHEL.) Sounds like someone's been telling stories. . . .

RACHEL: Daddy, you look at me if you are talking to me. I do not tell stories. We are a family. You don't tell stories when you're talking to family. Mommy said that all the time.

DAVID: Rachel, I know you mean well . . .

RACHEL: No, Daddy, this is for you. Because we are all worried about you. I'm sorry, but I think it's time you start talking with real women again. You can't . . .

DAVID: Let's just stop it right there, young lady.

RACHEL: Daddy, can't you see what's happening?

DAVID: What's happening is you are going to your room where you are going to think very carefully about what you just said. And you are going to think about privacy, and what that means. Do you understand?

(RACHEL *runs into the house,* ESTHER *following.*)

DAVID: (*Stopping* ESTHER) Esther, I can handle this without any more of your assistance. And my oh my, I wonder where Rachel picked up her new confrontational style?

ESTHER: She is saying what she thinks. If you would slow down enough to hear her, you would know that.

(DAVID *exits,* ESTHER *starts to follow.*)

PAUL: Mind your business.

ESTHER: This is my business.

PAUL: Esther, she's not ours.

ESTHER: I am aware of that. (ESTHER *exits into the house.*)

PAUL: (*To* CINDY) Heavy surf, young one.

CINDY: A minor squall, old one.

PAUL: Not so old.

CINDY: Not so young. (CINDY *sticks out her tongue.* PAUL *replies the same.*)

PAUL: They are all mad here / Save me and thee / And I 'gin to have / My doubts on thee . . . Looking forward to *school,* Cindy?

CINDY: Why don't you go beat up small children?

PAUL: You mean I'm not?

CINDY: You should have kids of your own to pick on. How come you don't?

PAUL: Don't what, you nosy little bug?

CINDY: You heard me.

PAUL: Well, Cindy, that decision is a highly personal and intimate choice between two people.

CINDY: Forget it.

PAUL: No, no, I'll answer your question. Because despite the difference in age between us, despite what some people might see as the difference in intelligence . . .

CINDY: Uh-huh.

PAUL: We trust each other, that's all I'm trying to say. Cindy, the reason Esther and I don't have children . . . God, this is painful . . .

CINDY: Then forget it.

PAUL: . . . The reason is—we were afraid they'd turn out like you.

CINDY: Yeah, yeah. You wouldn't be so nasty if you exercised.

PAUL: Whenever I get the urge to exercise, I lie down until it passes.

CINDY: It wouldn't hurt. You wouldn't be so . . .

PAUL: . . . toadlike, shall we say? You be nice or I won't tell you any more jokes.

CINDY: Such an awesome threat. Who's your friend?

PAUL: Oh, the wheels they are a-turning. Better ask all the pertinent questions before she gets back.

CINDY: I asked a question.

PAUL: (*Looking off*) She's turning around.

CINDY: Haven't you heard? Civilized people respond to questions.

PAUL: Do I detect a veiled threat in that over-glanded and muscle-bound young body?

CINDY: I could bust your transmission, if that's what you're saying.

PAUL: Kevin is my co-worker. Together we give money to the socially and artistically worthy.

CINDY: You do that?

PAUL: She does. I give money to those who bribe me, preferably with sexual favors.

CINDY: You're very gross.

PAUL: You're very cruel.

CINDY: (*Whispers*) Here she comes . . .

PAUL: (*Whispers*) Jealousy is a terrible thing in one so young.

CINDY: (*Whispers*) You want to sleep with the fishes? (KEVIN *enters.*)

KEVIN: Hello, again.

CINDY: 'Lo. (DAVID *enters from the house, picks up his towel, and notices* KEVIN.)

DAVID: I must give Esther credit. This is a big-league surprise.

PAUL: You remember . . .

DAVID: . . . Kevin, yes indeed.

KEVIN: Hello, David.

DAVID: Never forget distinctive appellations. One of my rules. (*To* CINDY) Appellation meaning . . .

CINDY: I know.

DAVID: (*To* KEVIN) Have you met?

CINDY: Cindy. Three times.

PAUL: I'll get our things in. (*Starts to go; to* CINDY.) Yoo-hoo?

CINDY: (*To* DAVID) Same time tomorrow?

DAVID: Well, it is pretty warm.

KEVIN: We could get up early.

PAUL: Another one. (PAUL *exits into the house.*)

KEVIN: If you're on the track by ten of seven . . .

DAVID: . . . you can lap the campus three times before the first bell.

CINDY: You two used to run together?

DAVID: Yes, we did.

KEVIN: Every other day for two years.

(PAUL'*s hand appears at the door, his finger pointing at* CINDY. CINDY *slowly exits.*)

KEVIN: So.

DAVID: So.

KEVIN: Look, David, I'd like to explain something.

DAVID: I wish you wouldn't.

KEVIN: Esther and Paul mean well, but I just learned that this is your wife's birthday.

DAVID: Please . . .

KEVIN: And I just learned how she died. I don't know why they couldn't have told me all this days ago, because I certainly wouldn't be here now. I thought I'd surprise you. I thought it would be funny or . . . I'm not sure what I thought. (*Pause*)

DAVID: Is that the explanation?

KEVIN: Yes. (*Pause*) And I'm perfectly willing to take the next boat out of here.

DAVID: Well, that seems a bit drastic, since you're here. Look, let me give you the tour, and you can decide if you want to stay. How's that?

KEVIN: All right.

DAVID: Well, we'll do Main Street and come back by the beach. But first you'll need to know where the waves come from. They begin in fetches.

KEVIN: Fetches?

DAVID: Fetches and roosts. . . .

(*They exit, and the lights slowly change.*)

Scene Three

(*Later that same afternoon. One by one the women enter in bathing suits. They spread towels and sun bathe, apply tanning creams, sun screens, zinc oxide, etc. All this is done slowly, without haste. The women smile to each other, but do not talk. Finally* PAUL *enters, fully dressed with a large hat. After a moment,* DAVID *enters. He surveys the scene, crosses to his weather station, and begins making notes in the bound log.*)

PAUL: (*To* DAVID) So, how long has it been?

DAVID: (*Still writing*) What?

PAUL: Since we saw you—months, right? Too long. You should come visit us more often. We'll go Chinese every night.

DAVID: We just got a Chinese.

PAUL: The Yankee Clipper Cantonese Inn and Gift Shop is not Chinese. I'm talking real ethnic, political refugees, I'm talking selection.

DAVID: We have a very nice selection.

PAUL: You've got to have the city, cradle of civilization. Rub up against the other animals.

DAVID: I'm fine right here.

PAUL: What about all the bustle, the give and take of the human comedy?

DAVID: No.

PAUL: Awfully quiet.

DAVID: Just the way I like it.

PAUL: Right. (*Searching for a newspaper clipping.*) I saved this for you.

DAVID: From the freak file?

PAUL: From last week's newspaper, in its glorious entirety. (*Reading*) Headline—Done in by Killer Hogs? Question mark? Chicago (UPI) The body of a night watchman was found yesterday in a hog pen at a South Side meatpacking firm, apparently eaten by the hogs. Name suppressed to avoid lawsuits, 32, was pronounced dead at Mercy Hospital. Homicide investigators said the victim's face and abdomen were severely chewed. They said about 100 hogs were in the pen and that the victim's clothes were hanging neatly on a nearby fence. An autopsy was scheduled.

DAVID: Let's hope so.

ESTHER: (*Still sunning*) Can't you keep them to yourself, just once?

PAUL: Oh, but it's so much better to share.

ESTHER: Uh-huh.

PAUL: (*Smiles at* ESTHER, *crosses to* DAVID, *who is still at the weather station.*) What's the forecast?

DAVID: Well, it's a close call, but I think we'll have weather today.

PAUL: That is reassuring. (*Sitting*) Hey, I ran into Belman the other day. Renowski has asked for an emergency leave of absence. I told Belman you were still available. He might call. (*Pause*) They would try to rearrange Renowski's schedule to accommodate you.

DAVID: Not interested, thank you. What happened to Renowski, anyway?

PAUL: Belman just said personal problems.

DAVID: Belman is always discreet. Renowski got caught with his hand up one too many pairs of panties, that's my educated opinion.

PAUL: It sounds like they'd really like you back. You could stay with us, overnight. You know that.

DAVID: I said no.

PAUL: Look, it might be good for you . . .

DAVID: What are you doing? No. Mind your business. (DAVID *returns to his weather log.*)

PAUL: Well, just a thought . . . (PAUL *returns to his reading;* KEVIN *crosses to* DAVID.)

KEVIN: It's a nice beach . . . And you've got a nice house.

DAVID: Thanks.

KEVIN: (*Pointing to the rain gauge.*) What's all that?

DAVID: Your basic thermometer, barometer, wind gauge. Helps me keep track of the elements. A bit of a hobby. (*Pause*)

KEVIN: How long have you been here, David?

DAVID: Ten years of summers, two year-round. We used to rent but there was a settlement after the accident. So, I bought the place.

KEVIN: And Rachel, is she happy here?

DAVID: Happy with the island? I think so.

KEVIN: Cindy?

DAVID: The indispensable companion and best friend. A bit like the maid in a French farce. (*Singing the theme from* Gilligan's Island) "So, that's the tale of our castaways / They're here for a long, long time . . .

KEVIN: And David?

DAVID: Oh, he's a slippery one, I'm told.

KEVIN: David, maybe I was just a face in the crowd . . .

DAVID: You were always a bit more than that.

KEVIN: Thanks. David, it's probably not my business, but I can't imagine you not teaching.

DAVID: Old Herman Melville and I, we've speared our last whale . . . just history now.

KEVIN: You made Melville, you made all of them dance in the air. And that's a rare gift.

DAVID: Like I said, just history now.

KEVIN: I know you'll get back to it.

DAVID: Look, what is all this about? This is really not your problem, is it?

KEVIN: No, it isn't. (KEVIN *begins to exit.* RACHEL *crosses to her.*)

RACHEL: Hi.

KEVIN: Hi.

RACHEL: Maybe after lunch you'd like to see the fleet get blessed?

KEVIN: Well, I'm not sure . . .

RACHEL: They have a band and they throw a cross into the harbor. It's fun. Are you hungry now or anything like that? There's a lot around. I know a great ice cream place. We can go right now.

KEVIN: Sounds fine.

RACHEL: And we'll make plans for tomorrow, okay?

KEVIN: Okay.

PAUL: (*Starting to go.*) The heavenly hash is on me. (*To* DAVID) You want?

DAVID: No.

PAUL: Esther?

ESTHER: Fudge ripple. (PAUL, RACHEL, and KEVIN *exit. Pause.*)

DAVID: Whose idea is Kevin? Yours?

ESTHER: Hers. And mine.

DAVID: I'm not sure what I'm supposed to say.

ESTHER: You're both adults. At least she is.

DAVID: Look, I didn't mean to snap at Rachel. Things just come out after I run.

ESTHER: You encouraged Rachel to spend the summer with us. What's the scenario today? Rachel betrayed poor old David and I'm cast as the witch abductor? If you didn't want Rachel to go you should have said so two months ago. And if you don't want us here, tell me now.

DAVID: You know I'm glad to see you. (*Pause*)

ESTHER: That's it? Thank you, Mr. Warmth. (*Pause*) What's your daily schedule now? Two hours of running and ten hours of television?

DAVID: You can do better than that.

ESTHER: I don't have to do better than that. You need to work. Your inactivity is destructive and irresponsible.

DAVID: Don't play the shrink with me, Esther, I'm not in the mood.

ESTHER: I'm not going to apologize for my training or my profession. You could benefit from therapy.

DAVID: Thank you, Ann Landers, for reprinting your columns.

ESTHER: Just short term, talking to someone instead of internalizing.

DAVID: God, you sound like the back of a matchbook.

ESTHER: You've got Rachel scared, do you know that?

DAVID: Let's not exaggerate a family spat, Esther. This morning was just parents and kids. It happens all the time.

ESTHER: Rachel is worried that you are withdrawing from her, and that scares her. That's what she and I talked about all summer. (*Pause*) Have you blacked out again?

DAVID: No. I run less, scout's honor. And I'm eating green vegetables. So don't throw Adele Davis at me.

ESTHER: Do you have pills?

DAVID. (*Shows bottle.*) Ingesting potassium has become a religious experience.

ESTHER: I mean sleeping pills.

DAVID: Play fair, Esther.

ESTHER: Do you?

DAVID: That was a mistake.

ESTHER: Taking half a bottle of sleeping pills on Gil's birthday was not a mistake. So don't make me ask again.

DAVID: No pills. (*Pause*) Does he know about last year?

ESTHER: Does who know?

DAVID: Paul.

ESTHER: I told you I told no one, or did you think I was just playing the shrink?

DAVID: Husbands and wives talk to each other. I seem to remember that.

ESTHER: You really don't have much of an opinion of me, do you? I told Paul and I told Rachel, no more and no less than what you and I decided. They came home from the movies and found you in the hospital with food poisoning. End of story.

DAVID: Thank you. (ESTHER *goes to leave.*) Esther! I just want her back. Nothing else.

ESTHER: Gil is not coming back. And you don't honor her memory by giving up on your own life. You're turning her into an icon, into something that has nothing to do with my sister.

DAVID: You truly have a vulgar little mind.

ESTHER: Maybe. Maybe I do have a vulgar little mind. And maybe I laugh too loud, just like my sister.

DAVID: Esther . . .

ESTHER: And I am proud of it all and you get no apologies from me.

DAVID: I didn't mean . . .

ESTHER: Oh yes, you meant. I can defend myself, but how dare you come down on Rachel, how dare you. You just take some of that mountain of pity you've built for yourself and point it at your daughter. When she was fourteen years old she watched her mother die. She watched her mother bleed to death. You just focus on that.

DAVID: All right . . . all right.

ESTHER: It took me a long time to like you, David, even longer to care, but I do care now. And if you throw your life down the toilet, I will cry for you, and I'll have a lot of bad nights.

You may not believe that, but it's the truth. But if you think I am going to let you take Rachel down with you, then you don't know who I am. Then you have never made the slightest effort to know who I am.

DAVID: I don't mean to exclude Rachel. It's just . . . I don't know if I can change.

ESTHER: Oh, but you can. Your life is happening now.

DAVID: No, Esther! Gil was my life. She was my anchor and without her I am lost. And the only way I have found something, some glue to hold the pieces together, is to sit on this beach and think of her, and what we had. So I sit here, and I remember. And that is how I have survived this last year. This is how I will survive this weekend, and how I will continue to survive. (*Pause*)

ESTHER: If that is the case, maybe Rachel should come back with us. Are you listening to me, David? I am not just talking about another summer vacation.

DAVID: I know. I'm trying to think.

ESTHER: What is there to think about? Leaving will be catastrophic for Rachel. She has friends here, school. David . . . Gil is not here any more. Rachel is. She is alive and hurting. Rachel needs you. You be her parent. Be her father!

DAVID: Don't you do that, Esther. You don't do that one. I'll take the mental hygiene lecture, but don't you talk to me about being a parent, and about sacrificing for my kid, because you don't know the first thing about it.

ESTHER: I just want you to remember who you are.

DAVID: I know damn well who I am. And I won't be told what it means to be a parent by someone who isn't one. Don't talk to me about my child and what she needs. At least I have one. And I can give you lessons on what it means to be a mother. (*Pause*)

ESTHER: I suggest we stop right here before things are said which cannot be repaired. Would you agree that we must do what's best for Rachel?

DAVID: Yes, I agree.

ESTHER: Good. We'll go to the cemetery tomorrow, put down some flowers, irises would be nice. Then we'll discuss this as a family.

(ESTHER *exits into the house.* DAVID *remains on stage as the lights shift to evening.*)

Scene Four

(*That evening. The lapping of the tide and the sound of wind passing through the rigging of boats is just barely audible.*)

DAVID: What's life? What's it cost? No . . . Who took the cookie from the cookie jar? (*Pause*) I said who took the cookie from the cookie jar? Damn it, who took the cookie from the cookie jar?

GILLIAN: You.

(GILLIAN *enters abruptly. She is in her middle thirties, dressed for the beach. Both stare at the water for a time, not looking at each other.*)

DAVID: Not me.

GILLIAN: Yes, you.

DAVID: Not you?

GILLIAN: Umm-hmmm. (No)

DAVID: Then who?

GILLIAN: Why, you!

DAVID: Me?

GILLIAN: Yes, you! You took the cookie from the cookie jar. (*Pause*)

DAVID: What's life?

GILLIAN: A magazine.

DAVID: What's it cost?

GILLIAN: Ten cents.

DAVID: That's cheap.

GILLIAN: That's life.

DAVID: What's life. Don't answer that.

GILLIAN: How's your dog?

DAVID: Ready for a romp.

GILLIAN: The correct response to "How's your dog?" is "Good, how's your dog?"

DAVID: I was always a bit slow.

GILLIAN: That part I liked. (DAVID *moves toward her.* GILLIAN *steps away.*) The waves are singing tonight.

DAVID: What do they say?

GILLIAN: That's a secret.

DAVID: You can tell me.

GILLIAN: They're singing life goes on.

DAVID: That's it?

GILLIAN: Life goes on and on.

DAVID: Profound, those waves.

GILLIAN: Mr. Cynic, Mr. Simple truths are never enough for you, Mr. Literature, Mr. Symbolism, . . .

DAVID: Enough.

GILLIAN: Mr. Book of the Month, Mr. PBS, Mr. S.A.T., Mr. . . .

DAVID: Enough! Enough. (*Pause*) Let the games begin.

GILLIAN: No games tonight.

DAVID: How about Great Apes and Baboons, always one of your favorites.

GILLIAN: No.

DAVID: Our little primate friends, come on.

GILLIAN: Read my lips. (*Mouthing 'n' 'o'*)

DAVID: How about an orangoutang?

GILLIAN: Maybe an orangoutang.

DAVID: Give us a young one, seeking acceptance into tribe.

GILLIAN: (*Imitates a young orangutan, picking at her clothes, cheeks puffed out.*) I prefer the young ones.

DAVID: Don't we all?

GILLIAN: You dirty filthy goat.

DAVID: I'm not a goat. I'm just a poor fisher boy lost on the shore.

GILLIAN: Oh, God, not this one again.

DAVID: If you could only help me, Ma'm, I'd be so grateful.

GILLIAN: How grateful?

DAVID: Oh, I'd do anything you might ask.

GILLIAN: Anything, my wild stallion?

DAVID: Stop it.

GILLIAN: You want Sister Theresa of the Little Flowers, or a real woman, with real passions?

DAVID: I think Sister Theresa might be quite relaxing.

GILLIAN: You get the whole package, my avenger, my little tug boat of love.

DAVID: Tug boat of love?

GILLIAN: Excuse me, Mr. Boundless wit. You need discipline, boy.

DAVID: Oh?

GILLIAN: We've been very moody lately, haven't we?

DAVID: What do we mean?

GILLIAN: We mean, snap at your own daughter like that, snap at *our* daughter.

DAVID: That was pretty bad. (*Pause*) Maybe we should have had another child. For balance. (*Pause*) Well, there was a lot happening back then. We both had careers. We couldn't . . .

GILLIAN: What do you mean "we", white man?

DAVID: We couldn't or we didn't want . . .

GILLIAN: One of us wanted another child.

DAVID: Yes.

GILLIAN: And one of us did not. (*Pause.* GILLIAN *points toward the sky.*) Northern sky, late summer, 47th latitude. What constellation? Can you take it, State University?

DAVID: (*Making buzzer sound.*) Cygnus, the swan.

GILLIAN: Correct. (*Imitating a swan, arms spread backward.*) Give that man . . . peace of mind.

DAVID: Yeah.

GILLIAN: That's your job, isn't it? (*Examining the house.*) She's a nice little house.

DAVID: Where we shall retire.

GILLIAN: That would have been nice. (*Long pause*)

DAVID: (*Staring at the house.*) The insurance covered everything, purchase price, points, buy back, even money in the bank. You were most thorough.

GILLIAN: I could build a quilt with all your guilt . . .

DAVID: (*Singing*) "Said Barnacle Bill the sailor . . ."

GILLIAN: You need toughening up, boy. All this misshapen, misapplied an-goo-ish!

DAVID: (*French*) "*C'est moi, c'est moi,* I'm forced to admit."

GILLIAN: Mr. Victim, Mr. Suffer-too-much! You need . . . (*Gesturing*) an infusion of zee life force!

DAVID: Not the life force.

GILLIAN: (*Looking in the direction where* KEVIN *exited.*) She's very . . . how shall I say? . . . very . . .

DAVID: . . . very ten years younger?

GILLIAN: That about covers it. I'm going to give you some pearls of wisdom, Bucky.

DAVID: Ah, pearls.

GILLIAN: Sex . . . You remember sex?

DAVID: How did it go again? Connect part 'A' to part 'B' . . .

GILLIAN: Sex is a normal, may I repeat n-o-r-m-a-l function of the adult primate, any primate. She seems quite nice.

DAVID: So you think . . .

GILLIAN: I just said what I think. (*Pause*) And watch your step with young Cynthia.

DAVID: What?

GILLIAN: The sap she's a-running in those veins.

DAVID: So?

GILLIAN: So? (*Pause*) And ease up on Rachel.

DAVID: Message received.

GILLIAN: Since when do you need me to . . .

DAVID: I said, message received. (*Pause*) What's life?

GILLIAN: I asks myself but I get no answers. (*Pause*) Gonna let you in on a secret, Bucky, just you and me.

DAVID: I like secrets.

GILLIAN: You may not like this one.

DAVID: Tell me anyway.

GILLIAN: The secret is, Bucky, I'm dead. Very . . . very . . . very dead. (*Long pause. Lights begin to fade around* GILLIAN). Got to go, Mr. Man . . .

DAVID: Don't go. What's life? What's it cost?

GILLIAN: (*Softly*) Ten cents.

DAVID: That's cheap.

(*The lights fade around* GILLIAN *as she exits.* RACHEL *enters.*)

RACHEL: That's life.

DAVID: What's life? Don't answer that question.

RACHEL: What are you doing out here, Daddy?

DAVID: Just catching up on the stars, kiddo. Virgo's rising and . . .

RACHEL: We have company.

DAVID: I know.

RACHEL: Who are you talking to?

DAVID: Come on now, kiddo, let's not have any eavesdropping. You know that sometimes I get a bit preoccupied.

RACHEL: You talk to Mommy, don't you? You come out here every night and talk to Mommy. And I'm not supposed to say anything, am I? It's like we've had this secret for a whole year. Daddy, some nights you are out here for hours. What am I supposed to think? That's why I had to go away this summer. I didn't want to have this secret. I don't want to keep hearing you and pretend that I don't. (*Pause*)

DAVID: I was pretty bad to you today, kiddo. I'm sorry.

RACHEL: Did you hear me, Daddy?

DAVID: Yes. I heard you, Rachel. Would you like to spend more time with Esther and Paul?

RACHEL: Do you want me to go back with them?

DAVID: I want you to be happy.

RACHEL: Daddy, please don't blame yourself for what happened on the boat.

DAVID: I'm trying, kiddo.

RACHEL: Daddy, I'd change things if I could, but I don't know how. If I could make it me who fell instead of Mommy . . .

DAVID: Now you stop that! You don't think that, ever, ever. You promise me that, right now.

RACHEL: I promise.

DAVID: You're my best girl, always and forever. I just want you to have what's best for you.

RACHEL: That might mean me going back with Paul and Esther. (*Pause*)

DAVID: I don't know. Maybe . . . (*Pause*)

RACHEL: You go walk. I know you have regular habits.

DAVID: (*Kissing her.*) Don't get cold.

RACHEL: I won't.

(DAVID *exits. After a beat,* GILLIAN *enters and moves slowly toward* RACHEL, *stopping when she is standing directly behind her.* GILLIAN *lifts her hand and points a finger skyward. A star falls, a sliver of light across the stage.* GILLIAN *points again, another star falls.* GILLIAN's *arms reach down over* RACHEL. RACHEL's *hands slowly reach up over her head. Slowly, the heads and hands of both become tightly wrapped, but not touching.* RACHEL *looks skyward. She is crying.*)

RACHEL: Happy birthday, Mommy.

(*Lights fade to black.*)

(End of Act One)

ACT TWO

Scene One

(*The beach, the following morning.* RACHEL *is sitting alone.* KEVIN *enters from the house.*)

KEVIN: (*Sitting, pointing to the ocean.*) What's out there?

RACHEL: Portugal, eventually.

KEVIN: You must be . . . a junior?

RACHEL: A senior. I skipped a year.

KEVIN: A brain, huh? Straight A's?

RACHEL: No. Well . . . almost.

KEVIN: College?

RACHEL: Oh, yeah. I like to study sciences.

KEVIN: Such as?

RACHEL: Anthropology, you know, primates? (KEVIN *nodding 'yes.'*) Orangoutangs, baboons, gorillas. And us, too, for all our big ideas . . . You know, there is this theory that we all come from the ocean.

KEVIN: Now that I've heard of.

RACHEL: No, no, later in the evolutionary cycle.

KEVIN: Oh.

RACHEL: We were already baboons, and we came out of our trees and we waded into rivers and tidal pools and we ate plants and caught small fish. Because we are omnivorous, you know that?

KEVIN: Right.

RACHEL: I believe it because if you look at the hair on your body (*Lightly tracing the hair on* KEVIN's *arm.*) when it's wet, every hair falls into perfect position to increase movement through water.

KEVIN: (*Looking at her arm.*) That's amazing.

RACHEL: It sounds so right, doesn't it? I mean, when you hear it explained like that you just know it has to be true. My mother thought that's how we got here. (*Pause*) The theory is totally discredited in biology journals.

KEVIN: Too bad. So you read biology journals?

RACHEL: If you're going to get where you want to go, you've got to know the information. My mother used to say that . . . I'm sorry.

KEVIN: What are you sorry about?

RACHEL: I shouldn't keep going on about my mother.

KEVIN: Wait a minute. Today is your mother's birthday, right?

RACHEL: Yes.

KEVIN: And you were very proud of her. And I think that is terrific.

RACHEL: She was a great anthropologist, really devoted to her work. She spent a lot of time in the field. That was hard. But I was real proud of her.

KEVIN: Those are the magic words for mothers. Mothers need to know their daughters are proud of them.

RACHEL: Even the strong mothers?

KEVIN: Every mother has this fear, this mindless fear . . . and when your daughter says "Mommy, I'm real proud of you . . ." Well, I have a little girl, and when she says that to me, that will be a red-letter day.

RACHEL: You have a little girl?

KEVIN: Yeah.

RACHEL: You should have brought her.

KEVIN: She's in good hands. Well, fairly good hands.

RACHEL: Do you ever need a babysitter?

KEVIN: Always.

RACHEL: Well, I could, if you wanted me to. I could give you some references. And I might be moving back to the city soon, anyway.

KEVIN: It's a deal. (*Pause*) How about you and I do something special, just the two of us?

RACHEL: Okay, what?

KEVIN: You're the native. You decide.

RACHEL: Well, there is this place, an old lighthouse. It's very special.

KEVIN: Sounds great.

RACHEL: We'll have to take the bikes.

KEVIN: Even better. (DAVID *enters from the house.*)

DAVID: (*To* RACHEL) Morning, kiddo.

RACHEL: Good morning, Daddy.

DAVID: (*To* KEVIN) Good morning.

KEVIN: Good morning, David.

DAVID: (*To* KEVIN) Sleep well?

KEVIN: Fine.

DAVID: No mosquitoes?

KEVIN: No.

DAVID: Air not too heavy? The island retains a lot of moisture. Makes the air heavy. That bothers some people.

KEVIN: Not me.

RACHEL: I'll go check the tires. (*Starting to exit.*)

DAVID: Rachel?

RACHEL: Yes, Daddy?

DAVID: Just . . . there's a lot of traffic. Just be careful. (RACHEL *exits.* ESTHER *enters.*) Good morning, Esther. (ESTHER *ignores him. To* KEVIN.) Planning an outing? (KEVIN *nods "yes."*) Am I invited?

KEVIN: No, just us ladies. (*Starting to exit.*)

DAVID: (*To* KEVIN) Maybe we could run a little later? For old times' sake?

KEVIN: Why don't you let me think about that?

(KEVIN *exits.* ESTHER *begins Tai Chi exercises, very slow, deliberate movements.* DAVID *crosses to his weather station, making notes in his log.*)

DAVID: Some day you will have to show me how to do that.

ESTHER: (*Still exercising*) Just routine and repetition.

DAVID: Esther, I said some things yesterday, that I'm not proud of this morning.

ESTHER: (*Still exercising*) Yeah.

DAVID: I'm sorry.

ESTHER: Fine. (*Pause*)

DAVID: Esther . . .

ESTHER: (*Stopping the exercise.*) What am I supposed to say now? It's okay, David? No harm done? I got slapped down. I got put in my place. Whether I have children, whether Paul and I have children, is a choice we've made, and I live with that.

DAVID: I know.

ESTHER: And you do not touch that without an invitation. And I'll tell you something else. I will not allow you to relive your arguments with Gillian through me. That is vulgar, truly vulgar. I will not give you that luxury.

DAVID: Esther . . .

ESTHER: Oh, David, I am so tired of hammering away at this wall you have built between yourself and the rest of us. For two years I have watched you turn yourself into a zombie, whose only friend is a sixteen-year-old girl. Or maybe she's a bit more than that?

DAVID: No, no she is not any more than that.

ESTHER: I am through, David. No more arguments, no more trying to reach you. If you want to play—what, Keeper of the Holy Grail—out here, just you and. I won't say Gillian, but whatever, then fine. I'm through. If you want it broken between you and me . . . just decide. And if you force me to fight for Rachel in court, I will. (*Starting to exit.*)

DAVID: Wait a minute. It doesn't have to come to that. Esther, I'm trying to talk to you. I don't know what else to say.

ESTHER: Well, maybe you could say, "Esther, how are you? Are you all right?" Maybe you could say, "Esther, I know you lost someone on that boat, too." Maybe . . . Maybe . . .

DAVID: (*Crossing to her.*) Hey, take it easy.

ESTHER: Oh, you stupid bastard. Today is the day she died and you and I are snarling at each other like two animals in a cage.

DAVID: (*Giving her his handkerchief.*) You can't fall apart. You're our rock.

ESTHER: Yeah, I'm one hell of a rock. (*Pause*) How did we ever let it get like this?

DAVID: I have this theory.

ESTHER: You would.

DAVID: We always talked to each other through her, saw each other through her. She was our buffer. Now there's just us.

ESTHER: Yeah. (*Pause*) You made her very happy.

DAVID: That was her.

ESTHER: You were the best thing that ever happened to her.

I got that from the horse's mouth. You made her very, very, very happy, you little turd. (*Pause*) I'm sorry it's not working out between you and Kevin. I guess I thought you needed a little . . .

DAVID: . . . shock treatment? Maybe.

(PAUL *enters, carrying a box of muffins.*)

PAUL: I have just survived something that made my skin crawl. I'm glad neither of you had to go through it. My hands are shaking.

DAVID: What are you talking about?

PAUL: I've finally seen the true face of your little island paradise. I was at the baker, innocently buying our daily muffins, you know, six blues, six crans, and a piece of peach cobbler which I have no intentions of sharing with anyone, when this crusty, barnacle-faced fellow, smelling like bilge, and, well, I'll spare you . . .

ESTHER: . . . I'm getting a bad feeling about this . . .

PAUL: . . . Well, he turns to me and he says: A church is looking for a bell ringer . . .

ESTHER: Run for cover.

PAUL: A guy comes in to the priest. He's got no arms, nothing. He says, "Father, let me ring the bells. I know I can do it." The priest is reluctant, but he figures he'll give the guy a chance. So they go up to the belfry, and before the priest can say a word, the guy runs against the largest bell, hits his face right against it, picks himself up, blam, right in the face. He's just about finished the Angelus, one note left. He runs, misses the bell, and falls a hundred feet to his death. The priest goes running down, there's a crowd all around. A cop comes up to the priest, "Father, do you know this man?" "No, I don't. But his face sure rings a bell." (*Pause*) A week later, another guy comes into the church, no arms, nothing. He says, "Father, all my life I've wanted to ring the bells, please give me a chance." Before the priest can say a word, the guy runs up the stairs to the bells. The same thing, he runs at the biggest bell, bang, right in the face . . .

DAVID: . . . he's on the very last note . . .

PAUL: . . . when he loses his footing and falls dead to the ground. The priest comes down, crowd all around. The cop comes up to him. "Father, do you know this man?" The priest shakes his head. "No, but I've got to tell you, he's a dead ringer for a guy who was in here last week." (*Pause*) Hey, what's up? You two haven't been fighting again?

ESTHER: (*Crossing to him.*) My hubby, I think I'll keep him. But I might have his larynx removed.

PAUL: (*Minus larynx*) . . . So the priest says, "No, but I . . ."

ESTHER: (*Pushing* PAUL *toward the door.*) Get inside before I hurt you.

PAUL: Why do you have to hurt me?

ESTHER: I don't have to hurt you. I freely choose to hurt you. Move. (PAUL *exits into the house. To* DAVID.) Let's eat.

(ESTHER *and* DAVID *exit into the house. After a beat* CINDY *enters, looks toward the house, then off stage.* KEVIN *and* RACHEL *enter,* RACHEL *with a bicycle pump.*)

KEVIN: Hi.

CINDY: 'Lo.

RACHEL: We're going on a little outing. Want to come?

CINDY: No. Thanks. No.

RACHEL: You sure?

CINDY: Yeah.

KEVIN: We might run a little later.

CINDY: Thanks, I've got things to do.

RACHEL: Things?

CINDY: Yeah, things, stuff.

KEVIN: I'll pack us a little something to eat. (*Exits into the house.*)

RACHEL: You can come with us, you know.

CINDY: I know.

RACHEL: Honestly, she doesn't even bite.

CINDY: I know. She's wonderful. She's great. You think he likes her?

RACHEL: Why don't you ask him?

CINDY: You don't ask things like that. (*Pause*) I think he likes her. I know he likes her.

RACHEL: And how do you know?

CINDY: I got the power. I know. He likes her.

RACHEL: If he likes her or she likes him, is up to them, isn't it? Well?

CINDY: Yeah.

RACHEL: So watch out for yourself.

CINDY: And what is that supposed to mean?

RACHEL: It means stop worrying about my father and whether he's happy and look out for yourself.

CINDY: I'm keeping myself invisible.

RACHEL: I don't want you to be invisible. I just don't want you to get hurt.

CINDY: Okay. I'll be visible.

RACHEL: Promise?

CINDY: Promise. (*Pause*) His name is Matthew.

RACHEL: Matthew what?

CINDY: Just Matthew. That's as far as I got.

RACHEL: Well, is he year-round or summer?

CINDY: He's new, but he's . . . permanent. And he's in our class.

(KEVIN *enters from the house, with a small brown bag.* PAUL *follows her.*)

KEVIN: We're all set. (*To* CINDY) You're sure you don't want to come?

CINDY: Yeah, no.

RACHEL: You sure?

CINDY: Yeah.

KEVIN: Okay, 'bye.

RACHEL: 'Bye.

CINDY: 'Bye.

(KEVIN *and* RACHEL *exit.*)

PAUL: Well, if it isn't a lost little swallow on the way to Capistrano.

CINDY: No, it isn't.

PAUL: Maybe a vulture returning to Hinkley, Ohio?

CINDY: What?

PAUL: It's true, every year, on the same exact day, a flock of vultures descends on a little town in Ohio.

CINDY: How come you know all this junk?

PAUL: I make it my business to know junk.

CINDY: Is David here?

PAUL: He's eating breakfast, to which you're invited.

CINDY: Eating? We're supposed to go running. (CINDY *starts to exit.*)

PAUL: Wait a minute. You can run later, can't you?

CINDY: Just forget it. (CINDY *exits.* PAUL *watches her leave, then returns to the house.*)

Scene Two

(*The foundation and decaying walls of an old lighthouse.* RACHEL *and* KEVIN *enter on bikes.*)

RACHEL: This is it. The sand has been silting up on this side of the island. So they moved the channel further out, and built a new lighthouse about forty years ago. This one's all deserted now.

KEVIN: Where's your house?

RACHEL: (*Pointing*) There. And that's Main Street, and the harbor. And over there is an old wreck, but you can only see it at low tide. It's pretty boring, anyway.

KEVIN: This is perfect.

RACHEL: I used to just sit here and think of this ocean going everywhere that people go, and people sitting on a beach somewhere, and looking at the water, just like us.

KEVIN: You think a lot. When I was your age, said Grandma, I thought about make-up and boys, and telephones and boys, and stuffed animals and boys. The stuffed animals gave me the best return on my time.

RACHEL: How about a muffin?

KEVIN: Sounds good.

(RACHEL *crosses to* KEVIN's *bike, opening the carry bag. She slowly pulls out an old baseball hat.*)

KEVIN: What did you find?

RACHEL: This was my mother's hat, kind of her lucky hat. The last time I saw her, I mean before the accident, she was wearing this hat. She always wore this hat. This was her bike. It's a long story.

KEVIN: I'm in no rush.

RACHEL: We used to come out here, first thing when she got back from the summer. It was like our place to get reacquainted, have a mother–daughter.

KEVIN: So this is a very special place.

RACHEL: Yes. She would tell me all about her orangoutangs and then she'd go develop her pictures. I remember the last time she had given the orangoutangs our names. Esther was the bossy one. Paul was the one that made faces all the time. And Rachel was very, very quiet. I had forgotten all that. You know sometimes I think about her, and I tell myself if I think about her, somehow she's still alive. That's crazy, right?

KEVIN: That's not crazy. That's miles and miles from crazy.

RACHEL: I went with her once, to Kenya, when I was nine. I was in her way the whole time, though she never said so. The next summer I lied. I said it was too hot, I wanted to stay on the beach. I could have helped her now. I know how to tag animals and I can do the weighing and the observing. We could have been friends. That's what she wanted.

KEVIN: How about you?

RACHEL: I just wanted her to be my mother. She was a good scientist. I think she was the best. But she was away a lot. And she took risks. Going up on that mast was reckless. It was stupid and reckless and why doesn't anyone talk about that?

KEVIN: I don't know, Rachel.

RACHEL: She shouldn't have gone up there. She was my mother, and if she had acted like my mother, just that one time, then maybe she'd be alive today.

KEVIN: Oh Rachel, I didn't really know your mother. But I know that sometimes we have to make some very difficult choices. You will, too. I think those choices must have been very hard for her. She had dreams and hopes for you, but she had some dreams for herself as well. And I think if she tried to make some of those dreams happen, then she must have paid a price, too.

(*Pause*)

RACHEL: I guess she did. Look, I don't want you to think I'm normally like this. I'm really pretty stable.

KEVIN: You're allowed.

RACHEL: I'm sorry Daddy wasn't friendly yesterday.

KEVIN: These things happen.

RACHEL: It's been rough on him. I guess this weekend wasn't fair to either of you.

KEVIN: Don't you worry about it.

RACHEL: He really does have some very good qualities.

KEVIN: (*Laughs*) I'll try and keep that in mind.

RACHEL: Look, I know we just got here . . .

KEVIN: Hey, I'm ready to ride.

RACHEL: I'll take you back by the north side.

KEVIN: Tell you what, I'll wait for you at the road.

RACHEL: Thank you, Kevin.

KEVIN: Anytime.

(KEVIN *exits on her bike.* RACHEL *remains behind for several beats, taking the hat out of the carry bag. She puts the hat back into the bag and exits. The lights gradually fade around the lighthouse.*)

Scene Three

(*The house, later that same afternoon.* PAUL *and* ESTHER *enter.* PAUL *carries the Sunday papers, sits, and begins to read.* ESTHER *carries a vase and several irises which she places in the vase. After a beat,* CINDY *slowly enters and sits on the deck.*)

CINDY: Hi, are they here?

PAUL: Who they?

CINDY: The people that live in this house.

PAUL: Oh, those theys, no. (CINDY *starts to exit.*) How about I get out the checker board?

CINDY: No, you're reading your paper.

PAUL: Great exercise, really builds up your fingers.

CINDY: No, thanks.

ESTHER: I'm going to make some lemonade, how about a glass?

CINDY: No, I'll head home, I guess.

ESTHER: Come in and have some lemonade. You can help me make it.

CINDY: Okay.

(ESTHER *exits into the house, followed by* CINDY, *who makes a face at* PAUL, *who returns to his paper. After several beats,* KEVIN *enters, running flat out.*)

KEVIN: (*To* PAUL) Good-bye, get lost, get out of here right now.

(PAUL *picks up his paper, exits into the house.* DAVID *enters, winded from running.*)

DAVID: God, you've been practicing.

KEVIN: You always sprinted the last hundred yards.

DAVID: But you never did, not fair.

KEVIN: Just waiting for the right moment.

DAVID: That's quite a kick you have there.

KEVIN: (*Stretching*) And don't you forget it.

DAVID: Brings back the old days, you run, you teach, you run . . . Kevin, I'm sorry about yesterday.

KEVIN: Oh?

DAVID: I was rude to you. And I am sorry.

KEVIN: I'm glad to hear that, David.

DAVID: So . . . fill me in.

KEVIN: Not much to tell. I found someone. He found me. We were happy for a time. Then like the continents we drifted imperceptibly apart.

DAVID: A very modern story.

KEVIN: (*Pause*) I have a little girl, Clair. She is four years old, about this tall (*Gestures*) and is the most intelligent and insightful child in the universe.

DAVID: Where is she now?

KEVIN: She's with her father. She's with . . . What is his name?

DAVID: Oh yes, old what's-his-name.

KEVIN: It begins with an "r".

DAVID: Richard . . . Raoul . . . Rasputin . . .

KEVIN: Robert.

DAVID: Robert.

KEVIN: Mm-hmm. As in Robert the perfect mate, as in Robert the envy of all my women friends. Attentive, thoughtful, and sensitive was Robert. And a good cook. Oh, I miss the magic he could create with a piece of veal. And he did the dishes, and the laundry, helped with the bathroom, exterminated stray insects.

DAVID: The dirty jobs.

KEVIN: To give him credit he was good with vermin. And he had interesting friends. He was very . . . modern. Never an argument, never a disagreement, never an emotional ambiguity not pinned to the wall and examined in squirming detail. He called that being honest.

DAVID: That can be a chore.

KEVIN: If it was in him it was good and it was to be explored, regardless of consequences. He was so open, so vulnerable, so . . . so. One day he said, "Let's have another child." "Yes," I said. Three weeks later he told me he was seeing someone else, and he knew it would not be honest not to communicate that to me and he hoped it wouldn't change things between us. I hit him. That was honest. And threw him out. I spent a lot of time by myself, minus Robert's interesting friends. I beat up several Nautilus machines, snarled at the few men who had the misfortune to cross my path, and eventually got him out of my system.

DAVID: It never quite works out the way you imagine.

KEVIN: No, it doesn't. So now I'm in the market.

DAVID: Oh?

KEVIN: The man market.

DAVID: Oh.

KEVIN: So I accept market conditions.

DAVID: But you'd like a warranty, dependable service.

KEVIN: Something along those lines. (*Pause*)

DAVID: When you finally . . . got him out of your system, was it a sudden moment, bright lights, music playing?

KEVIN: More gradual, I think. But somewhere along the way I jumped.

DAVID: Jumped?

KEVIN: Look, it's just one woman's opinion, okay? But I think you reach a point where you're ready to come back into the world, have some fun, do some living. You're still angry or annoyed or whatever it is, but you jump back in. With some luck, someone will catch you.

DAVID: And if no one does?

KEVIN: You land on your ass. (*Pause*) But you're back in. But you've got to want to.

DAVID: You know a lot.

KEVIN: I know a little about jumping, that's all.

(PAUL *enters from the house.*)

PAUL: (*To* KEVIN) Hello.

KEVIN: Hi.

PAUL: (*To* DAVID) Esther's gone to find Rachel. We thought we'd go to the cemetery now.

DAVID: Of course. Right, I forgot. I'll go change. (*To* KEVIN) Tan, don't burn. (DAVID *exits.*)

PAUL: So?

KEVIN: So?

PAUL: What you expected?

KEVIN: I don't know what I expected.

PAUL: Then not what you expected?

KEVIN: It has to be either or?

PAUL: Just classifying, the male imperative. Changed?

KEVIN: Yes, changed.

PAUL: Older?

KEVIN: Younger, in some ways.

PAUL: That's unnatural.

KEVIN: He seems so . . . uncertain.

PAUL: A man of his time and civilization . . . Two guys walk into the local bar . . .

KEVIN: No.

PAUL: . . . There's a pregnant kangaroo behind the counter . . .

KEVIN: No! You and I are going to take a little walk.

PAUL: What for?

KEVIN: You're going to tell me about Gillian.

PAUL: Do I have to?

KEVIN: Oh, I think so.

(PAUL *and* KEVIN *exit. The lights slowly change to evening.*)

Scene Four

(*Evening. The stage is empty. A heron calls, solitary and mournful. From the house* ESTHER *and* PAUL *enter carrying citronella candles which they light and spread about the deck. Another bird calls as* DAVID *enters, pausing for a moment to listen to the birds.* CINDY *and* RACHEL *enter and sit on the beach.* CINDY *carries a backpack.* KEVIN *enters with a tray of drinks.* CINDY *removes a bottle of wine from her bag.*)

CINDY: (*Reading label*) *Liebfraumilch.* My brother says it means jumping woman milk. You want to get trashed?

RACHEL: No.

CINDY: You're supposed to get trashed when summer ends.

RACHEL: I'll get you a glass.

CINDY: No! You don't use a glass. You swill. Like this. (*Drinking*) If this island is supposed to be so sophisticated then how come it doesn't even have a mall? I've yet to hear an answer to that.

DAVID: (*Responding to a surge of bird calls.*) Smauk.

ESTHER: Smauk, smauk.

(GILLIAN *enters from the beach.* DAVID *is momentarily confused.*)

GILLIAN: Smauk.

ESTHER: Smauk, smauk, or I'll make you talk . . .

DAVID: Anything is better than orangoutangs.

PAUL: Smauk, smauk, smauk . . . (*Pause*)

DAVID: Smauk.

(RACHEL *crosses to the deck and sits.*)

ESTHER: Once, when we were kids . . .

GILLIAN: . . . Gillian got to go when Mother gave blood . . .

ESTHER: (*To* RACHEL) Your grandmother was a fanatic about giving blood, every two months . . .

GILLIAN: Drip, drip . . .

ESTHER: Something about the orphans in Armenia. I was seven, in the second grade, aggrieved that I couldn't go.

GILLIAN: Gil was five . . .

ESTHER: . . . the baby. And as mean-tempered, nasty, and stubborn a baby as . . .

GILLIAN: . . . *Anyway* . . .

ESTHER: . . . God, I used to love to beat her up.

PAUL: Dominant traits always emerge early.

ESTHER: You want to walk again, buddy?

RACHEL: What about the story?

ESTHER: Anyway . . .

GILLIAN: Anyway, Gil went with Mommy.

ESTHER: And when they got back I asked her, what happened?

GILLIAN: And Gil said, "Mommy laid down on a big boat and they covered her with a big white sail. And they sailed away to a magic land and took her picture. The end."

ESTHER: I'm still trying to figure that one out.

RACHEL: (*To* ESTHER) Tell the one about the watermelon.

ESTHER: You've heard that one.

RACHEL: Again.

ESTHER: Oh . . . okay.

GILLIAN: Once upon a time . . .

ESTHER: . . . we went camping, in the wilds, all of us. Now at this time . . .

GILLIAN: . . . your grandfather was . . .

ESTHER: . . . a little difficult to get along with.

DAVID: Easy now.

ESTHER: Shall we say . . .

GILLIAN: . . . difficult to please. Anyway . . .

ESTHER: . . . Anyway. Gil was nine, I think.

GILLIAN: Eight.

ESTHER: With little skinny legs like sticks. Real ugly kid.

RACHEL: Tell the story.

GILLIAN: Anyway, Gil was wading in this little stream, doing nothing at all, and she . . .

ESTHER: . . . found . . .

GILLIAN: . . . this . . .

ESTHER AND GILLIAN: . . . watermelon!

GILLIAN: Now you gotta understand . . .

ESTHER: . . . that no one in our family ever found anything . . .

GILLIAN: . . . let alone watermelons in the stream of life.

ESTHER: So she picked it up and started to carry it back to the shore, holding it in her scrawny little hands thinking . . .

GILLIAN: . . . "I have found a watermelon. I'm going to be happy for the rest of my life."

ESTHER: "My daddy will love me."

GILLIAN: "Everyone will love me."

ESTHER: Then this guy from the next campsite came running along the shore. Huge, beefy guy with his beefy wife next to him.

GILLIAN: Enormous.

ESTHER: Huge, a walking mountain. Think of . . .

PAUL: . . . Orson Welles in Bermuda shorts.

ESTHER: And he's screaming . . .

GILLIAN: . . . "Police, Police. Don't drop my watermelon."

ESTHER: So we had to give it back.

GILLIAN: And Daddy didn't talk to me the whole week. And

when I went on my first date, sweaty and nervous and ten years older, he said, "Don't get into trouble, and don't bring home a watermelon."

KEVIN: (*Crossing to* CINDY.) Hi.

CINDY: 'Lo.

KEVIN: Can I join you?

CINDY: Sure, pull up some beach. (KEVIN *sits.* CINDY *shows her the wine bottle.*) Would you like some? I'm getting ready for school.

KEVIN: It was the best of times, it was the worst of times. It was high school. (*They toast.*)

CINDY: There's something I've got to ask you.

KEVIN: What?

CINDY: Why are you called Kevin, anyway?

KEVIN: Oh, my parents wanted a boy, and they didn't get one.

CINDY: Yeah, parents are just like that.

GILLIAN: (*To* DAVID) She seems quite nice. (*Long pause*)

DAVID: "We are ashamed of conversation."

PAUL: Robert Penn Warren in *Three Darknesses.*

ESTHER: Mr. College Bowl.

PAUL: And the bonus question?

ESTHER: I'll give you a bonus question. A toast.

PAUL: To Gillian.

DAVID: To Gillian.

RACHEL: To Mommy.

ESTHER: Who would be, who is, thirty seven years young. (*Pause*)

KEVIN: (*To* CINDY) When I was a kid, I kept my name a secret.

One year I was a Debby. Then Sheila. I got as far as Lolita, then I just went with Kevin.

CINDY: I think it's a wicked name.

KEVIN: Wicked excellent?

CINDY: Wicked excellent.

KEVIN: Come visit me.

CINDY: Are you serious?

KEVIN: You can check out the big, bad world. Come with Rachel. I'll whisk you around.

CINDY: Okay.

ESTHER: (*Going into the house with the tray of glasses.*) Goodnight.

PAUL: (*To* DAVID) See you in the morning. (*Exits into the house.*)

GILLIAN: Tonight's my birthday, Bucky, and I want a present. How about a little small talk?

DAVID: (*To* KEVIN) Goodnight.

GILLIAN: That wasn't it.

RACHEL: (*To* KEVIN) Goodnight.

KEVIN: Goodnight. (*Goes into the house.* CINDY *remains on the beach, apart from the others.*)

GILLIAN: Oh, you're not listening, Bucky, and you are forgetting things about me and about our daughter. I don't know how else to do this. (*The stage lights abruptly shift.*) We've got to strike a bargain tonight. No games, no jokes. Just a real bargain between you and me. All I have worked for, every dream, every hope, is in this grant. I have it in my hand, David, twenty-one and published in the field. And let's face it, even though you're good at it, Hawthorne and Melville won't ever do much more than pay the rent. So, please, don't ask me to do it all. Now I will have this child, since you're so set on it. Oh, I know that when it's here and I hold it in my arms, it will be a miracle and a wonder, and a thousand other things. But right now . . . Oh, David, I'm just not ready to be a mother. So here's the bargain. Once the kid is here, it's yours. You feed it, you do the baths, the diapers, all of it. And starting next summer, I get to do my work, no questions asked. And if you can't accept this, if this isn't good enough, then I will get in the car, drive to the city, and take care of this tonight. So, lover, we have our bargain, don't we? (GILLIAN *slowly exits down the beach.*)

DAVID: (*Crossing to* RACHEL.) How's my girl?

RACHEL: I'm okay.

DAVID: We have some deciding to do, Kiddo.

RACHEL: I know.

DAVID: Have you thought any thoughts?

RACHEL: I asks myself, but I get no answers.

DAVID: Kiddo, sometimes I forget things, real important things. I think because I missed your mother so much, I forgot just how important you are to me, and how much I love you, and how much I need you. (*Pause*)

RACHEL: You know what I remember, Daddy, the first thing I remember as a baby?

DAVID: What's that?

RACHEL: Me sitting and looking up at your face, your hands holding the side of my head, very soft and very strong. Daddy, it was always you who took care of things, and I'd like to be there for you, if I can. Then when you miss Mommy, or when I miss her, we could talk about it.

DAVID: Yeah, I'd like that.

RACHEL: And if it doesn't work out, then maybe I'll go to Aunt Esther's.

DAVID: And that would be okay.

RACHEL: But let's try, Daddy, all right?

DAVID: All right.

RACHEL: Because we are a team.

DAVID: Right.

RACHEL: (*Whispering*) And from now on, I'll keep the star charts, okay?

DAVID: Okay.

RACHEL: Can we tell Aunt Esther?

DAVID: You go ahead. I'll round up the strays. (*They embrace. RACHEL goes into the house. DAVID crosses down to CINDY.*) Come join us, Cin.

CINDY: It's late. I should get back. (*Doesn't move*)

DAVID: Another balmy island evening. (*Notices bottle*) Now what would mother and father say?

CINDY: Don't smoke. No drugs. No hard stuff. And never, ever, ever get in a car with a drunk driver.

DAVID: Sound advice. (*He sits.*) But there's no need to drink alone.

CINDY: I wasn't alone. Kevin drank most of that. She's pretty decent, I guess. Are you two getting friendly? I mean are you . . . I mean I . . . You must think I'm real stupid.

DAVID: No, I don't think that at all. I don't really know Kevin very well. It's confusing. Sometimes you want and you don't want, all at the same time. I guess it's not so different at thirty-seven as at sixteen. In fact I think you can be more confused at thirty-seven—you've had more time to practice. But I do want all of us to be friends, no matter what. Especially you and me.

CINDY: Okay.

DAVID: (*Taking bottle and drinking.*) You know, Cin, one thing my wife used to tell me is that I take people for granted. I think maybe we, I mean I, take you for granted.

CINDY: Oh, no. You're always great to me.

DAVID: I hope so. You're a good friend to Rachel and you've been a good friend to me. Just running with you, talking, sitting and watching the waves come dancing in from their fetches, that's been a big help. Thank you.

CINDY: You're welcome. (*She is crying.*)

DAVID: Hey, what's all this?

CINDY: I don't know.

DAVID: Stand up. (DAVID *stands.*)

CINDY: What?

DAVID: On your feet. (CINDY *stands.*) Now close your eyes. Now, are you listening to me, Cindy?

CINDY: I am . . . I'm . . . just, just don't tell me I'm real young and I'll get over it and I'll find some stupid boy because I don't want to get over it. Oh, shit! (CINDY *starts to exit,* DAVID *holds her.*)

DAVID: You stay right here. I mean it. Eyes closed? (CINDY *nods "Yes."*) Now I want you to count to ten, quietly. And when you stop I want you to turn around and go home. And I want you to come back in the morning and we'll run in the sand, and look for shooting stars. Now start counting.

CINDY: (*Eyes still closed.*) I already did.

DAVID: Well, count again. (CINDY *counts.* GILLIAN *does a bird call.* DAVID *kisses* CINDY.) Keep those eyes closed. Now get out of here.

(CINDY *turns, eyes still closed, and exits. The lights fade out.*)

Scene Five

(*The following morning.* DAVID *is sitting on the beach. After a beat* PAUL *enters with luggage, his attaché case, and* ESTHER's *beach bag.*)

PAUL: Well, we're off.

DAVID: On the road again, huh?

PAUL: We thought we'd get a jump on the traffic. (*Pause*) So you walk up the beach . . .

DAVID: Then I walk down the beach. That about covers it.

PAUL: You would make a great punk rocker—you're so into monotony. Ever get sunstroke?

DAVID: Not me.

PAUL: Look, we've known each other for twenty years.

DAVID: So?

PAUL: In all those twenty years I never once intervened in your life. Never offered even the most casual suggestion. And I usually use my nose to sniff out truffles, like a good little piggy. I do not normally go sticking it where it has no business. (*Pause*) I called Belman. I didn't "just bump into him." You're a bright boy; you figured that out. I heard about the Renowski business. They were going to circle the wagons, exploit some graduate students, whatever it is they do, just to cover the schedule. I asked Belman if I could talk to you, usher you back in.

DAVID: Look, I didn't . . .

PAUL: Let me finish. I've thought a lot about this. Some nights I think about nothing else. David, if it had been me and not you. I mean Esther and not Gillian, I would be going just the way you're going. It's not my business, I know . . .

DAVID: Paul . . .

PAUL: I would have withdrawn, too. Chuck the job. Because if she was gone, Christ, I'd be nothing without her. And I'd blame myself, just like you. Look, I don't go for all this men have feelings crap, never have. And all this honest speaking of the emotions, all I see it's given us is a nation of John McEnroe clones. But this is the closest I can get to it. I care about you, worry about you. If I was over there, I think I'd have snapped, done damage to myself. I have three friends, total, and I worry. Look, I love you. So knock it off! Don't spend another winter like the last one, punishing yourself in all this natural beauty. Take the damned teaching position. Entertain some strange children. Occupy your mind. Do it as a favor to me. Or do it as a penance for being such a pain in the ass. I don't care how you think about it, just do it. And this is me talking, not Esther. And when it's over, if nothing has altered, you can hold this against me when we're all old and wrinkled. (*Pause*)

DAVID: What if I told you I've had a chance to think things through overnight, and I decided to take the job on my own?

PAUL: Oh, no, this was to be my one unreasonable demand, and I wanted all the credit. (*Pause*)

DAVID: Okay.

PAUL: Okay what?

DAVID: Okay, I'll take the position.

PAUL: Yeah?

DAVID: You're not exactly asking me to swallow cut glass, you know.

PAUL: You're serious, not just humor me now, screw me later?

DAVID: It's obviously a good thing for me to do. So I'll do it.

PAUL: So all this gushy stuff works?

DAVID: Maybe. (*Pause*)

PAUL: It all seems a little anticlimactic.

DAVID: I can't help you there.

PAUL: You're not going to yell or scream.

DAVID: No, but I won't throw my racket, either. Paul, thank you.

PAUL: You're welcome. (ESTHER *enters, dressed for the beach.*)

ESTHER: Hi there, sailors, looking for a good time?

PAUL: (*Crossing to her.*) His master's voice.

ESTHER: (*Looking from* PAUL *to* DAVID.) You two been having a little man talk?

PAUL: You know, the usual. Are Jockey shorts really more comfortable than Fruit of the Loom? That kind of thing.

ESTHER: Right. (*To* DAVID) We thought we'd stop off at High Surf. You want to come along?

DAVID: In a minute.

ESTHER: (*To* PAUL) Rachel may be showing off a young gentleman. So clod behavior is out.

PAUL: Act like a clod, *moi?*

ESTHER: You have been warned. (*To* DAVID) You okay?

DAVID: I'm okay. Just give me a minute.

(ESTHER *and* PAUL *exit.* DAVID *is alone on one side of the stage. The lights shift as* GILLIAN *enters from the opposite side. Neither looks at the other.* DAVID *slowly points to various parts of the sky.*)

DAVID: Regulus. Arcturus. Denebola. Alkaid. Hamal. Mirach. Capella. Procyon. Ruchbah. Mizar. And Vega, where planets are coming to life, even as we speak.

GILLIAN: The man who can call down the stars from the heavens, that man will I have, that man shall I make my own, to have and to cherish . . .

DAVID: Till . . .

GILLIAN: . . . death . . .

GILLIAN AND DAVID: (*À lá Yul Brynner*) ". . . Et cetera! Et cetera!"

DAVID: Oh, so hard to balance, the "was" and the "is."

GILLIAN: And the what may be. Ann Landers says . . .

DAVID: . . . women mourn . . .

GILLIAN: . . . and men replace.

DAVID: It ain't necessarily so.

GILLIAN: The waves are singing tonight.

(GILLIAN *abruptly jumps on to the corner of the deck. She points herself forward, hands behind her back, moving from side to side.* DAVID *stands directly in front of her and moves in the same rhythm.*)

DAVID: I wish you wouldn't do that.

GILLIAN: Play with your wheel. I'm not bothering you.

DAVID: It's stupid. It's childish. It's dangerous. And it's reckless.

GILLIAN: You're such a pussy.

DAVID: Would you come down?

GILLIAN: Pussy, pussy.

DAVID: If I say that to you I'm a stinking porky pig, but you can say anything you want to me.

GILLIAN: You finally figured it out.

DAVID: Get down!

GILLIAN: I love it when you try to get emotional.

DAVID: I am not trying. I am getting very pissed off.

GILLIAN: Hmm. Vulgarisms, I love it. More.

DAVID: You're behaving like a spoiled little brat.

GILLIAN: What?

DAVID: You stupid bitch, get down!

GILLIAN: Sorry pal; life is for extravagance!

(GILLIAN *spreads her hair out behind her. At the same time they both "hit" something.* GILLIAN *flies off the deck, jumping into* DAVID's *arms.*)

DAVID: Gil! (*The lights abruptly shift back to morning.*)

KEVIN: (*From offstage*) David! (GILLIAN *slowly exits.* KEVIN *comes in through the gate, casually dressed for the beach.*) I'm sent to fetch the car keys. (*Pause*) And to fetch you.

DAVID: Right, yes. Right.

KEVIN: (*Starting to go.*) You want to be alone right now?

DAVID: No. Have a seat. (*They sit.*) I want to ask you a question.

And you don't have to answer. The question is, what were you looking for, coming out here?

KEVIN: You mean this, you and me?

DAVID: You don't have to answer.

KEVIN: But life is short, so I will. (*Pause*) I'm looking for someone who might be kind. I didn't get too much kindness on my last ride. So I thought you . . .

DAVID: . . . might be kind?

KEVIN: Yes.

DAVID: Why?

KEVIN: Well, I guess I think people who have had great losses either become kind, or they go bad. And I was willing to take my chances.

DAVID: Ah. (*Pause*) I'll probably be getting into the city once in a while, in fact fairly regularly. Not that I didn't get in anyway, to buy books or stamps. I mean for my collection, which I'll show you some time, though most people are bored to tears by stamp collections. I think of them as tiny art forms, like posters, well, if I was in town I thought . . .

KEVIN: We could meet for . . .

DAVID: Wait, wait, don't you do the asking.

KEVIN: It's not right if the woman asks the man?

DAVID: In the great scheme of things I don't think it matters who does the asking. But in this little scheme, here, it matters that I do the asking.

KEVIN: Okay.

DAVID: Right. Well, if I'm in town and you're in town then maybe we could meet for dinner or something. Well, what do you say? (*Pause*)

KEVIN: (*Thinking it over.*) Hmmm . . . well . . . yes. Of course, David, dinner.

DAVID: Or a movie?

KEVIN: A show?

DAVID: A museum.

KEVIN: A something. (KEVIN *kisses him.*) I've been waiting a long time for that.

DAVID: Oh, really? (DAVID *kisses her. After a beat,* RACHEL *enters.*)

DAVID: Hello.

RACHEL: You don't have to stop. I just need the car keys, to load the trunk.

DAVID: Right. (*Starting to exit.*) Consider it done. Be right back. (DAVID *exits. Pause.*)

KEVIN: This must be a little strange for you.

RACHEL: No. Well, maybe a little. Must be strange for you, too.

KEVIN: Pretty strange.

RACHEL: I hope it's not too much for you. 'Cause when I asked Aunt Esther to call you . . .

KEVIN: Wait a minute, you what?

RACHEL: Well, I asked Esther to get someone like you. I hope you don't mind.

KEVIN: (*As she exits.*) I'm flattered.

(RACHEL *remains on stage. After a beat,* DAVID *enters, humming the theme from* Gilligan's Island.)

RACHEL: Daddy, I've got something for you. (*She removes GIL-LIAN's hat from her back pocket.*) I found it in Mommy's bike.

DAVID: (*Taking the hat.*) Thank you. It's going to be a real scorcher today. (*He puts the hat on* RACHEL's *head.*) How's your dog? (*He hands* RACHEL *the car keys.*)

RACHEL: Good. How's your dog?

DAVID: Good.

RACHEL: Good.

(RACHEL *exits.* DAVID *remains on stage. As the lights gradually fade to black, he exits.*)

(Curtain)

PRESET

Act One

Stage: Chairs on marks
Table on marks
Shirt on back of SR chair
Towel on railing
Sand on porch and under chairs
Telescope on marks above log
Star chart on marks DC
Planosphere, Star log, Star book, pencil, and
    flashlight on Star chart
Glitter on sand

Lights: Work lights out
Q 5 up (5 ct.)

Sound: Backstage monitors working
Headsets working

Backstage: Q lights working
Reverse Q lights working

Act Two

Stage: Chairs on marks
Table on marks
Strike broom, rag, stamp magazine
Open house door

DEATH in the POT

by Manuel Van Loggem

An English style thriller with a fascinating plot that takes intricate twists and turns, as a husband and wife try to kill each other off, aided by a mysterious Merchant of Death. Four males, two females; single interior set.

LOOKING-GLASS

by Michael Sutton and Cynthia Mandelberg

This provocative chronicle, interspersed with fantasy sequences from ALICE IN
WONDERLAND, traces the career of Charles Dodgson (better known as Lewis Car-
roll) from his first work on the immortal classic, to his near downfall when accused
of immorality. Six males, four females with some doubling; either simple fluid staging
or elaborate sets can be used.

One Acts ~ And ~ Monologues ~ For ~

Women

BY~LUDMILLA BOLLOW

These haunting plays mark the arrival of a new voice in the American Theater.
This volume consists of two thirty to thirty-five minute monologues and a forty
minute one-act for two women. All three call for simple interior sets.

A musical presentation of magical and possible events in the lives of two women born in the last century. A minimum of three males and four females, though it can be expanded to accommodate a great number; may be done with simple fluid staging. A piano vocal score is available for perusal or rental.

This delightful small scale musical is about the life of Gilbert and Sullivan. It is interspersed with some of the best known songs from the Savoy operas, including THE PIRATES OF PENZANCE, HMS PINAFORE and THE MIKADO. This show had a very successful run on the West End of London in 1975. Five males, three females, though more actors may be used as "stage-hands" and chorus members. Settings may be fluid and simple, or complex. A piano vocal score is available for perusal or rental.

SAGA

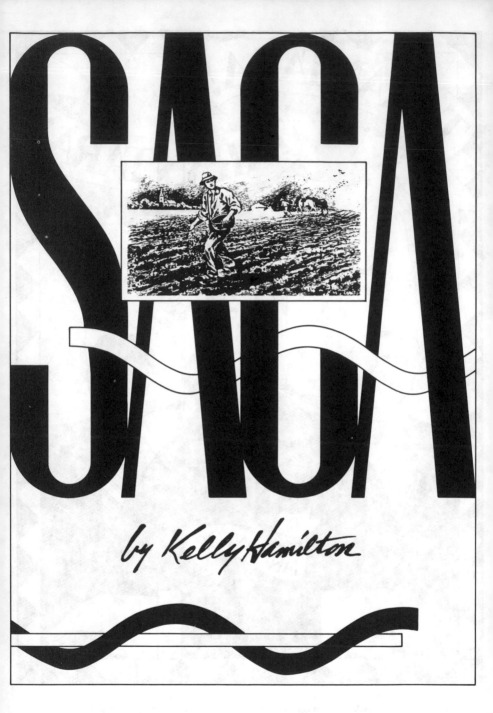

by Kelly Hamilton

This wonderful musical is a history of America's pioneers as they push their way across the country. A minimum of eight males and eight females are necessary, and the show can be expanded to use many more actors. Settings can be fluid and simple or elaborate. A piano vocal score is available for perusal or rental.

SOME RAIN

by James Edward Luczak

Set in rural Alabama in 1968, the play is a bittersweet tale of a middle-aged waitress whose ability to love and be loved is re-kindled by her chance encounter with a young drifter. Two males, one female; single interior and exterior set.

BATTERY

BY DANIEL THERRIAULT

Electricity is the central metaphor and an expressive image for this unusual love story set in an electrical workshop. This young playwright has been compared to Sam Shepard and David Mamet for his superb use of language. Two males, one female; single interior set.

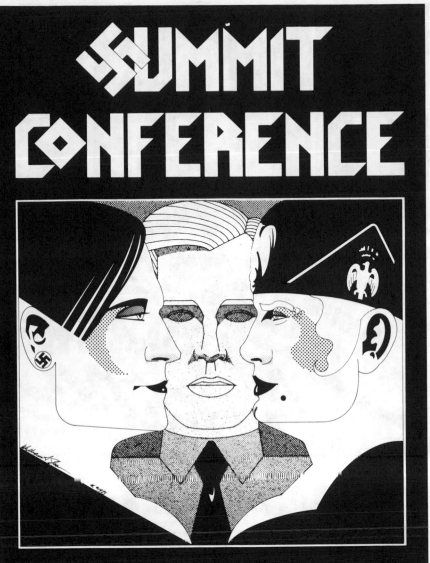

SUMMIT CONFERENCE

ROBERT DAVID MacDONALD

Set in the Berlin chancellery in 1941, this play is a fictional encounter between the mistresses of Hitler and Mussolini: Eva Braun and Clara Petacci. This show had a successful run on London's West End in 1982 with Glenda Jackson. There are some restrictions on production rights.

This volume contains three of the dynamic shows created by members of the Omaha Magic Theatre: **Megan Terry**, Jo Ann Schmidman, Marianne de Pury, Lynn Herrick and John J. Sheehan. AMERICAN KING'S ENGLISH FOR QUEENS, RUNNING GAG, BABES IN THE BIGHOUSE are all shows that call for more females than males, and have simple flexible sets.

ESCOFFIER
KING OF CHEFS
by
Owen S. Rackleff

©Tom V.H.

In this one-man show set in a Monte Carlo villa at the end of the last century, the grand master of the kitchen, Escoffier, ponders a glorious return from retirement. In doing so, he relates anecdotes about the famous and shares his mouth-watering recipes with the audience. One male; single interior set.

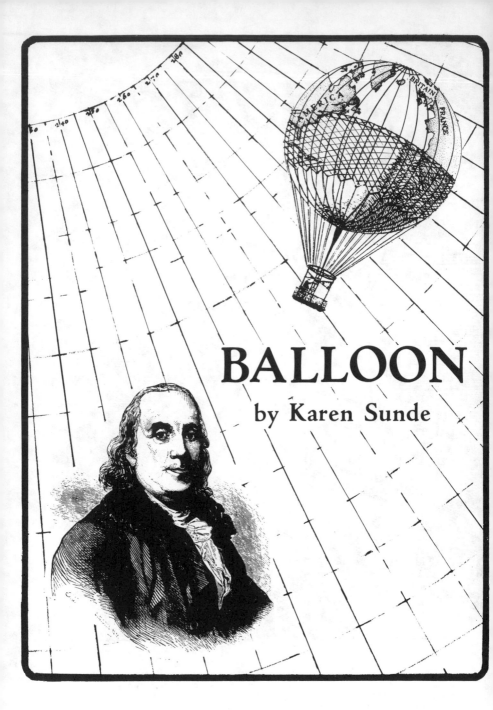

BALLOON
by Karen Sunde

18th century Paris is the setting of this structurally inventive play about Benjamin Franklin and his French contemporaries. Five males, one female; single interior set.